RIBS

RIBS

A Connoisseur's Guide to Grilling and Barbecuing

Text by Christopher B. O'Hara
Photographs by William Nash

THE LYONS PRESS

This book is for Christopher John O'Hara. I wrote every word for you.

Printed in Mexico

Design and Composition by A Good Thing, Inc.

10 9 8 7 6 5 4 3 2 1

Library of Congress Cataloguing-in-Publication Data is available on file.

Contents

Ribs: An Introduction

When I first approached Tony Lyons, the publisher of this book, about doing a book on ribs, he seemed skeptical. "What does a guy from Long Island know about barbecue?" he asked. It was a legitimate question. Most people think barbecue to be the exclusive domain of those crusty Southern practitioners—those ageless, photogenic pitmasters who seem to have barbecue sauce running through their veins and innate knowledge of the Pit.

I first got bitten by the barbecue bug when I was in college. I went to Atlanta to visit a good friend of mine, Randy Moore. It was the kind of trip where I had just about enough dough for the plane ticket and a six pack of beer. We managed to go out for dinner one night, however. Due to a fairly "relaxed" college curriculum, Randy had a fair amount of time on his hands to explore cost-effective dining options around town. He promised to take me to a place with real barbecued ribs that "just fell off the bone." We arrived at a residential street about two miles outside of Atlanta proper. One particular home had about fifteen cars parked in front of it. "Here we are," Randy announced.

"What do you mean?" I asked. There wasn't a restaurant in sight.

"That house," said Randy, "is the best barbecue restaurant in Georgia."

And so it was. Owned by an elderly Black couple, the house's living room was filled with ten small tables that sat four, each fully occupied and filled with brimming plates of barbecue. We sat down, and didn't even have to order. About five minutes later, two brimming plates of baby back ribs appeared, along with sides of collard greens, hush puppies, and the blackest baked beans I've ever seen. The tab was $15 for both of us. I left a $10 tip with the stipulation I could get the recipe for those ribs—I was going to impress my friends back in New York.

"You can't get the recipe, honey," said our hostess, "but you can meet the cook. He's my husband."

Squirreled behind the house was a dimunitive, chubby, seventy-five-year-old man sweating over a steel barbecue pit made from an old oil drum. We chatted for about a half hour, and I soaked up ample amounts of Dixie beer and barbecue knowledge. Later that week I returned home and promptly burned my first rack of baby back ribs.

Years of practice and experimentation on the old black Weber Kettle at my family's summerhouse yielded better and better results. The secret to cooking great barbecued ribs is there is no secret. It's really easy! Once you figure out how to slow-cook them, and master a few simple sauces, you are on your way.

All right, so I'm a white New Yorker; perhaps the diametrical opposite of what most people picture when they think "barbecued ribs." My Yankee heritage will probably preclude me from winning a blue ribbon at the "Hogmasters Bar-B-Que Cookoff" in Pigknuckle, South Carolina. But I accept that. And I'm here to tell you that good barbecue—and really good barbecued ribs in particular—can be made by anyone. In fact, you can make amazing "authentic" barbecue without having spent years behind the barbecue shack mixing sauces and tending the Pit.

The best part about ribs is they become a hobby. Most of the fun is about preparing the different marinades and sauces you'll use. Preparing some of them will remind you of your first "cooking experiments" when you were a kid—basically, chuck everything you can find into a pan and turn up the heat. "Hey, Mom, look what I made!"

Ribs is going to show you how to be a master barbecuer in the limited field of rib cooking. Almost every recipe in this book can be experimented with and modified. Have fun in your backyard this year, and have fun experimenting!

RIBS

Chapter One
Ribs: A Connoisseur's Primer

A few millennia ago, a few minutes after the discovery of fire, a cave in the depths of central Africa was the birthplace of man's greatest achievement. Picture if you will, the smelliest, largest Neanderthal you've ever seen carving into a gnarled and equally hairy piece of meat and laying it on an open flame. That's how man's love affair with grilling started. With a few minor exceptions, it hasn't progressed much in the last thousand or so years.

That's why *Ribs* isn't a fancy cookbook with a lot of complicated instructions and obscure words in it. There are lots of color pictures, though. (Keep in mind that what you will make won't look anything like the pictures. At all.) However, this book will teach you enough cool recipes to make you a virtuoso of many open-flame cooking techniques, and fill your mind with enough trivial yet fascinating facts that your friends will think you're a backyard Confucius. For example: Did you ever stick an open can of beer up a chicken's ass? You just might after you read this book (see Drunken Chicken, page 84).

Grilling Versus Barbecuing

There's one thing you should know before I begin, and if you already know this, please accept my apologies, because I only recently learned it myself. Grilling and barbecuing are two separate things. Grilling is the act of rapidly cooking something directly over an open flame. Barbecuing, on the other hand, is the act of slowly cooking something without the flame coming in contact with the food (indirect heat).

So, when we go to the garage and get out the "Bar-B-Que Kettle" to grill some hamburgers, it gets mighty confusing. Most of us have a grill, no matter what the manufacturer calls it. And most of the cooking we do is pure grilling (steaks, hamburgers, and so on). However, when we slow-cook chicken over low-burning embers, what we're doing is barbecuing. The distinction is important because the cooking techniques are vastly different, giving different results. But more on that later (see Chapter 4: Rib Cooking Techniques).

If You Can Cook It, You Can Cook It Outside

One of the greatest joys of barbecuing—and perhaps the most important factor in our love affair with it—is the fact that we can do it outdoors. This is especially relevant to the married man, who is generally more appreciative of the opportunity to escape the house, even if the trip takes him no further than his driveway.

Of course there's more to the love of barbecue than the chance to slip out of the house. Often you'll hear people remark that something "always tastes better when you cook it on the grill." I think this sentiment has more to do with memories of summers past than the wonderful charcoal taste from a good slab of barbecue. The barbecue grill rarely seems to come out unless there's a party or big gathering—so I think it's natural to associate grilled food with good times.

Another reason we love outdoor cooking so much is the fact that it stirs something inside us that screams "authentic" or "real." Much of the food we eat every day is either prepared for us by somebody else, or comes out of a box or a can. When we pull the barbecue out of the garage, we are making a commitment to cooking in its most basic form. This is the reason people grill—there is nothing in the world that can replicate the taste of properly grilled or barbecued food. We can't get it out of a microwave.

Chapter Two
The Gear

Gas or charcoal? This question often stirs a debate that is no less complex and fraught with partisanship than a presidential election. And, like politics, the "facts" that pervade the argument are often based less on truth than ideology. For example, many die-hard charcoal grill adherents insist that they just can't get that "real barbecue flavor" from a gas grill. Conversely, gas grill owners—loathe to give up the convenience of a flip-switch ignition—argue that charcoal grills are inadequate because they can't control temperature easily during cooking. Both are right. But first let's separate the truth from the fiction.

Flavor

You know that wonderful charcoal flavor you get when you bite into a perfectly grilled hamburger that's a bit crunchy on the outside, and wonderfully moist and tender on the inside? A lot of folks say that the flavor comes exclusively from cooking over a charcoal fire. I think that's true to a certain degree, but generally wrong.

That flavor we all know and love comes from the cooking process itself. Fat drippings from the meat fall into the grill's innards, and are returned in the form of smoke that flavors the food. That's what creates "charcoal" flavor. Real charcoal is wood, which gives it some absorbency even when it's red-hot. That means charcoal tends to emit more flavor during the cooking process than the metal slats beneath a gas grill's cooking surface. So there's naturally more flavor from charcoal. However, gas grills have become much more advanced today, incorporating ingenious slanted "flavor bars," which capture drippings and create flavorful smoke, all while funneling grease into a manageable tray for disposal. Additionally, there are many types of prepared woods and grill seasonings that can be added to both types of grills to enhance cooking flavor.

Convenience

In this category you'll find a lot of reasons to purchase a gas grill over a charcoal grill. First, gas grills are a real time-saver. With your old charcoal grill, you have to drag the grill out, clean any ashes out of the bottom, fill it with charcoal, stack the coals properly to get a good light, soak the charcoal with smelly lighter fluid, let it sit for a few minutes, light it, wait about a half hour to get a good charcoal surface, redistribute the coals, and place the grill on top. All this preparation can take up to an hour. With a gas grill, you simply have to turn it on.

My advice on the timeworn gas versus charcoal question? Have both. I do, and I can't tell you how grateful I am. I have a beautiful Weber gas grill that I use when I'm lazy or have a lot of guests who I need to feed quickly and without hassle. And I have a 1943 model "Eclipse" aluminum charcoal grill that I take out when I really feel like putting personal attention into my cooking—or, when I need to add seasoned wood to the fire to slowly barbecue chicken. (I also have three Weber Kettles, all in different sizes, at my summerhouse, but that's due to the fact that I won't let anyone throw them out, and I'm a little sick in the head when it comes to barbecues.)

But there are important convenience issues to consider with a gas grill as well. For example, what do you do when you're suddenly out of propane on a Saturday night with a houseful of hungry guests expecting your famous barbecue ribs? (This happened to me last summer.) You're basically screwed. You can't run to the 7-Eleven and pick up a spare tank of propane. With a charcoal grill, all you need is to get a big bag of Kingsford briquettes. Another thing to mention here is that gas grills are machines, which—like all machines—have a tendency to break. Not so with charcoal grills, which are essentially any open area covered by a grill.

Price

Any discussion of charcoal versus gas has to include price. Unless you are prepared to make extreme sacrifices in basic quality, you can't step into a gas grill for less than $500, and even that will get you the most basic model. Very effective and high-quality charcoal units, by comparison, can be had at a starting price of under $100. This comes down to lifestyle choice, and a few questions need to be addressed when making the decision to purchase a grill. Ask yourself: Am I planning to move in the near future, and will I take the grill with me? How often will I use the grill? Do I have adequate storage space for it? Will the grill spend the entire time outdoors, or do I need one that is easily moved from place to place? Depending on your needs, there is a grill for you in every price range, and for every use.

If you grill about once a month, for example, you may want a small, inexpensive charcoal unit that won't take up a lot of garage space and is easy to lug out twelve times a year. If you grill a few times a week, however, you may opt for a gas model substantial enough to stay on your patio year-round. If you are a real do-it-yourselfer, you may want to build a freestanding permanent grill in your backyard or attached to your house. Whatever you do, make sure you buy or build enough grill. Because you can never, ever, have too much grill.

Choosing Your Grill

The proliferation of so many different types of grills in every different size and price range on the market today is staggering. There's a grill for every taste and budget, ranging from as low as $20 to over $10,000. Your choice should come down to your own personal cooking habits. If you cook lots of steaks and burgers, you probably need the quick convenience of an easily lit gas grill. However, if you only break out the barbecue on special occasions to cook for large get-togethers, you might opt for a large charcoal unit. If you use the grill at home more than the oven, you probably want a permanent freestanding grill.

Here's a look at the various attributes of several different types of grills, especially in the context of rib cooking.

Size Matters

First of all, there is no such thing as the "perfect grill," although a lot of wannabe Emerils out there will try to convince you otherwise. I have a Weber gas grill, which I consider to be the perfect size for everyday grilling applications. Of course, I also live in a house that has a garage. Two years ago, that grill wouldn't have been very useful on the microscopic "deck" in my equally microscopic 18th Street apartment. Back then, I had a tiny Weber Bar-B-Que Kettle (which could fit two rib eye steaks perfectly). Obviously, you need a grill that meets your needs.

If you are an avid entertainer, for example, you need a grill that can accommodate food for around ten to twelve people at a time, preferably one with a large cooking area and some elevated racks for simultaneously grilling vegetables. However, if your entertaining is more one-on-one, you might opt for a more convenient, smaller grill that gets started—and cleans up—more quickly.

The Charcoal Grill

I think a discussion of charcoal grills without mentioning the greatest model ever built, the Weber Bar-B-Que Kettle, would be like a discussion about basketball without mentioning Michael Jordan. The Kettle is the hallmark in Weber's long and distinguished history of grill manufacturing. Shaped like a backyard UFO, the Kettle has probably grilled more hamburgers over its history than any other grill in the world. It's a very simple unit, and that is its beauty.

First, the Kettle can accommodate a feast on its large grill—about fifteen decent-size hamburgers, or about six half chickens, or a half of a butterflied leg of lamb with potatoes on the side. Second, the grill holds its heat like a dengue fever victim. The low-lying charcoal grate provides a generous, well-ventilated charcoal surface underneath the grill, and even a heavy buildup of ashes cannot stifle heat production.

The greatest attribute of this beloved grill is its accessible price: around $90. You simply can't buy more reliability, even if you spend hundreds more. My large black Kettle at the summerhouse was there when I was born—that's over thirty-one years ago! I think last year my uncle finally broke down and replaced the grill on it.

But why not just use a gas grill for the convenience? There are several good reasons. First, it is very difficult to smoke ribs properly using a gas grill (in fact, it's hard to "properly" smoke ribs on a regular charcoal grill too, but it can be done). Most of us don't have a proper smoker, so the charcoal grill is the next best thing. With gas grills, your heat source is predetermined; flames are going to come from those little holes in the gas pipes underneath, and that's it. With a charcoal grill, you have better control over your heating surface, but less control over the heat itself. You can arrange the coals to provide indirect heat so that your ribs cook without direct heat—an impossibility with a gas grill. To cook by indirect heat, all you need to do is place an aluminum pan about the size of a dinner dish in the middle of the coal tray, and pour the coals around it. Plus, charcoal grills add that crucial element in cooking ribs: flavorful smoke, and lots of it!

Charcoal grills also allow you a wide range of choices in fuel. You can burn lump charcoal, charcoal briquettes (charcoal, sawdust, and sand, bound together with a petroleum-based substance), or wood. Charcoal grills also enable you to add flavor to the fire itself—a decided advantage over gas grills. The addition of hardwoods (mesquite, hickory, or fruitwoods) or even fresh herbs (especially rosemary, thyme, fennel, and bay leaves) give you an extra flavor source complimentary to whatever marinade and mop you use. And there's nothing more appealing than the smell of ribs smoking over hickory fire.

There are a few disadvantages. During a long session of cooking, you will undoubtedly have to add and remove charcoal to maintain a steady heat. In fact, the phrase "steady heat" can never be applied to charcoal grilling—you're going to have to deal with hot spots on the grill that burn parts of your food. This can be a real problem with ribs where the cooking goal is "slow and low" for many hours at a time. The best solution is to find a unit that has a grill that can be easily removed (with food on it) during the cooking process. Or find a grill that has a trap door for adding coal underneath while you cook.

Charcoal barbecuing is a lot of work. But it's worth it.

The Gas Grill

As much of a barbecuing purist as I am, I still have a gas grill. When it comes to grilling hamburgers, steaks, or chicken, a gas grill is the clear choice: just flip it on, and off you go.

Gas grills provide a steady, even flow of heat through propane gas, a very clean-burning fuel. Because it's so clean-burning, it obviously doesn't add the smoky flavor that comes from charcoal or wood. To create that "charcoal" flavor, gas grills employ a system that allows fat to drip down and return to the meat in the form of smoke to create flavor. Many grills use lava rock to catch drippings; newer grills use a system of slanted "flavor bars" that catch drippings while conveniently funneling them into a fat-catching tray.

There are decided advantages to cooking ribs on a gas grill. Since the goal is slow-and-low cooking, gas grills make it easy to cook at low temperatures for hours at a time without having to add fuel. Additionally, when you're ready to sear on the last coating of sauce, you can crank up the heat without the hassle of adding more fuel and waiting for it to ignite.

The disadvantages are many as well. The only way you can add wood chips or other flavoring agents to the fire is by means of a aluminum pan—if you're lucky enough to get it to fit below the grill. Also, some gas grills make it tough to slow-cook meats because of the proximity of the grill to the heating elements.

Smokers

For ribs, the best piece of equipment you can own is a smoker. Smokers are fairly simple contraptions that are designed for one thing: cooking meats slowly over long periods of time. There are basically two types of smokers: Fire (also called offset) smokers and water smokers. The staple of good Southern barbecue, the offset smoker can be any covered unit that allows meat to be cooked indirectly by the smoke generated from burning hardwood. The units usually are large enough to contain a fairly good-size fire, which is reduced to embers. The grill should be "offset," allowing the meat to stay away from direct heat. The key to offset smoking is having a door that lets you add and remove fuel, so you can effectively "manage" your fire.

Water smoking is an innovative, compact way to achieve the same result. Because most people don't have the room to accommodate an ungainly wood smoker, the fairly compact, efficient water smoker has increased in popularity. The design is fairly simple: burning wood chunks heat water to boiling, the vapor from the water joins with the smoke from wood, coating the meat. The smoky vapor acts as a basting agent, keeping the meat moist and tender while flavoring it.

Smoking is the ideal way to cook ribs (and whole chicken, and lots of other whole meats that benefit from extended cooking periods). If you have the room and a few extra bucks lying around, I would definitely consider purchasing one; you won't regret it!

Accessories

Barbecuing wouldn't be as popular as it is if you had to sear your fingers over a piping hot grill every time you flipped a burger. That's why accessories— and stores like Brookstone— exist. These days you can find specialty grill accessories just about anywhere items for the home are sold. Here's a look at some essential—and not so essential—gear for your grill.

Tongs

Next to the grill itself, tongs are the most versatile piece of equipment you'll need. I'm talking about your run-of-the-mill $4.99 pair of stainless steel tongs; the kind you'll most likely find in restaurant kitchens. The reason so many professional chefs favor a

decent pair of tongs above all other cooking implements is their versatility. By acting as an elongated set of heatproof fingers, the proper set of tongs feel just as comfortable flipping a 1/4-pound hamburger or the most delicate filet of flounder. They are perfect for moving vegetables around the grill, plucking frankfurters off the grill, and the perfect steak flipper as well. Naturally, they are the perfect tools for managing racks of ribs (and single ribs) on the grill. The curved interior surface of the tong replaces that spoon you've been using to baste the meat with the marinade while it's cooking. Once you really get comfortable cooking with them, prodding the closed ends of the tongs into your steak will give you a better indication of temperature than your fingertip—and they make it less painful too!

Also, there's no better tool for organizing a dinner plate. Ever try to transfer a pot full of string beans or asparagus onto eight dinner plates with a slotted spoon? It makes a mess, and you can never get them to line up the right way. Just grab your tongs and pluck them out of the pot, let them drain, and artfully set them down neatly in a row, on the side of the plate. There are probably three or four different utensils you can throw away once you have a decent set of tongs.

Fork

The long-handled barbecue fork should only be used for one thing: moving really enormous items around the grill. I'm talking about big chickens and roasts. You'll see a lot of people use these two-pronged forks to stab into a steak to flip it. I think this is the worst thing you can do to a $9.00 rib eye steak or porterhouse cut. Even though it seems as if the hole you put into your meat disappears once you turn the steak over, this isn't the case. Grilling is all about quickly searing the outside of the meat, and locking in the juices so you retain moisture and tenderness. Everywhere you poke a hole into that steak, you're letting heat in and moisture out. If you happen to be a fidgety cooker, like me, you're apt to fill that steak with more holes than Sonny Corleone at a tollbooth. You are better served to use your tongs.

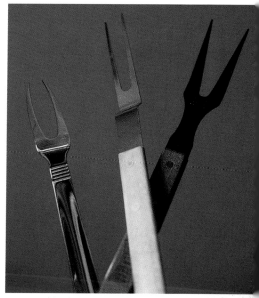

Spatula

There is perhaps no utensil more associated with the barbecue than the time-honored spatula: the all-in-one burger flipper, fly swatter, and grill scraper. A lot of companies are selling those oversize three-foot-long spatulas that look like they could double as a squash racket. I think these are great for keeping your hands out of the fire, but I have yet to find one with a nice, thin, flexible spatula at the end, which is the key to this tool's usefulness. No matter what you do, or what type of grill you have, you're going to encounter a piece of meat that basically seals itself onto the grilling surface, and no matter how you poke or prod it, the meat just doesn't want to leave the grill. Many times, jamming one of those thick-ended spatulas underneath the meat can tear the entire bottom off (the good, charcoaled part) just when the meat's ready to be served. I advocate finding a cheap, long-handled spatula with a thin, flexible end—the kind that you can work under a piece of meat, and get its thin, knifelike edge to work under the meat without tearing it apart. And don't go for a multipurpose spatula—the one with a serrated edge and a bottle opener on the handle. Always use the correct tool for the job. We all have a Swiss Army knife, but you've never seen anybody use the Phillips head screwdriver on it around the house, right?

Knife

There is no single utensil that will mark you as a slack-jawed barbecue novice faster than a long-handled "grill knife." These are serrated knives meant for cutting directly on the grill, and usually sold as part of a total utensil set. You're probably wondering why there's such an abundance of social stigma attached to the seemingly harmless grill knife. Here's why. Even if you are barbecuing for the very first time, and have not the slightest inclination what temperature your steak is while it's cooking, you should never, ever cut into it to find out.

Why?

Not only does this near-sacrilegious act immediately enjoin you to the ranks of boorish barbecue amateurs, it also makes a very indemnifying statement about yourself that—even if you are cooking with nobody else around—can serve as a source of deep, personal shame. It says, "I am going to ruin this beautiful porterhouse steak because I am too stupid to figure out how to grill it." (See Chapter 4 for methods to test meat temperature and "doneness.")

There is a place for a knife in barbecuing. That place is in the kitchen.

Brush

This essential utensil may be the diametrical opposite of the grill knife, in terms of imbuing its user with a certain amount of barbecuing respectability. Unlike other "gadgets" whose use suggests the uncertainty of their user, the brush—even while wielded by a rank amateur—lends the proper atmosphere of drama to the art of cooking. The right grill brush is vital to creating genuine barbecue, especially for slathering on rib mops (see below).

Barbecued foods thrive on marinade before—and especially *during*—the cooking process. That makes having a tool for transferring liquids smoothly over a surface vitally important. There is no better implement for this than a brush. And not necessarily a grill brush. In fact, here's another case where I recommend not purchasing a long-handled specialty grill utensil.

If you've ever been in a paint store, you know how paintbrushes can vary in quality. You have your throw-away $2.99 brush with nylon bristles (which tend to begin falling out of the brush even before the job is done); and you also have your $15.99 China bristle brushes with the nice wooden handle—the kind that, with proper care, will last forever. With the specialty barbecue brush, you're paying for all that wood in the handle, not the quality of the most important part: the brush itself.

That's why I advocate purchasing a really nice, expensive, two-inch-wide China bristle brush for your barbecue. This kind of brush spreads a really thick Texas–style barbecue sauce as well as a thin, vinegar-based North Carolina marinade. You can clean it with a light solution of dish soap and water, just as you would use to clean off latex paint.

Mop

You want to be a real pro? Consider using the traditional Texas "mop," a sauce utensil that looks just like its namesake. Texans actually use a mop to apply a thin, marinating barbecue sauce (also known as a "mop") during cooking.

Apron

There are some obvious advantages to donning the traditional apron for tending the barbecue, but none that immediately come to mind. Let's face it, only hardcore barbecue freaks will go so far as to tie on the "Hot Stuff" apron with a yard full of friends and family. However, realize that by sporting the humble cotton garment known as the "barbecue apron" you are honoring a tradition of cuisine that goes back centuries. Even if it does say, "Give Grampa Some Love."

I'm a tremendous fan of the apron for several reasons. First, I tend to over-exaggerate at the grill, especially when applying marinades. The apron probably saves me from a minimum of three shirt changes every time I barbecue. Second, I know the secret of the apron. It conveys authority and less says, "I'm in charge of this grill." That is important.

You know how Uncle Bob likes to come over to the barbecue and dispense annoying advice, or maybe even move a few items around while you're in the kitchen helping your wife? Once you start sporting the apron, all that will cease immediately. Without realizing it, old Uncle Bob will start treating you with more respect around the grill, and maybe even offer to get you a cold one while you're cooking.

Chapter Three
Rib Basics

There are five different types of ribs discussed in this book, each one with its unique — and tasty—qualities. Unless you're a butcher, you really don't need to know the technicalities of what exact part of the animal your ribs are from, but it can't hurt to know the basics.

Baby Back Ribs

Baby back ribs are the most popular type. Baby back refers to pork ribs, not beef. "Baby" merely refers to their size, as compared to the giant beef back ribs. Generally, baby backs cost the most because they are somewhat meatier, and therefore leaner than other ribs. The meat comes from the loin (that's the "back" part), which is considered one of the better cuts of pork (think tenderloin.) Baby backs are generally the most versatile ribs to cook. You can parboil and grill them, smoke them, oven-cook them, or

braise them, and they go with just about any type of dry rub, glaze, or barbecue sauce. If you can get to a decent butcher, buy your baby backs fresh. You will be surprised at how much better they are than the ones from your local supermarket. A note here: you'll notice that your baby backs will have a thin membrane of cartilage on the underside. You should always remember to remove it before cooking. (The same applies to all the other ribs discussed).

Beef Back Ribs

Beef back ribs, are obviously much larger than baby backs. They also tend to be a lot fattier. They are also quite delicious cooked slowly in the oven or smoked for long periods of time, which helps break down the meat, making them more tender. I'm a big fan of these ribs, especially smoked for a long, long time over a natural hardwood like hickory. They also seem to go best with a good tomato-based Texas–style sauce—the spicier the better. I generally like to serve these only to the family because not only are beef ribs generally considered to be of a lesser quality than pork baby backs, their enormous size makes them rather cumbersome to eat with any sense of decorum. But if you have the kind of friends I have, go ahead and chow down with abandon. You can always go outside and hose down afterward, and that's half the fun.

Spareribs

Spareribs are most closely associated with Chinese cuisine, and I tend to choose them from the butcher only when I'm going to prepare them Oriental–style. But that's just because I tend to lack imagination sometimes. The fact is, spareribs are just as good as baby backs; they have plenty of meat, but are marbled with a little more fat. I suppose if you are the type to prefer a rib eye steak to filet mignon, you will prefer spareribs to baby backs. Like baby backs, spareribs refer only to pork, so unless you want to be laughed out of the butcher store, don't go asking for any "beef spareribs." I don't know why they are called "spare" ribs . . . it's not like the poor pig could really spare them in the first place. I do know that they are from the side of the pig right next to his belly, which is where the phrase "side of ribs" comes from. If you get them from a butcher, he'll probably ask you whether or not you want the skirt—that extra flap of "mini ribs" attached to the side—left on or taken off. It's up to you, but I usually keep it on and gnaw on them later.

Country-Style Pork Ribs

Country-style pork ribs are hardly ribs at all. They come from the rear end of the pig, between the loin and the rib cage. The only thing that would lead you to believe that these are ribs at all is the tiny rib bone left behind in the end. They tend to be very thick, with lots of tender meat that's great for fork-and-knife eating. The trouble is getting them that way, since they can be notoriously tough unless cooked properly. I like to let them marinate for hours on end, and then either slow-smoke them or slow-cook them in the oven. They are the "poor man's tenderloin," but can be a very elegant dish when prepared correctly.

Short Ribs

Short ribs come from our friend the cow, not the pig. They are kind of similar to country-style pork ribs in that they are a "poor man's" dish because they come from the lesser cuts of the steer: the chuck portion (where hamburgers come from), and the bottom portion of the rib cage (like the country-style ribs). Unless you have Job-like patience in the cooking process, these ribs are going to be tough. And I mean shoe-leather tough. I love these ribs—when somebody else makes them for me. For my money, if I'm going

to spend four hours slaving over a smoker, I'll be preparing baby backs or maybe even beefback ribs. Of course, there is a better way to get these ribs nice and tender, and that's to slice them thin and allow them to marinate for a long time. As you will note on page 65, Korean Short Ribs can be some of the most tasty and tender ribs of all if you know the secret to preparing them.

Of course there are as many different types of ribs as there are edible animals. One Thanksgiving when I was working in Colorado as a snowmaker, my boss, who had recently "got his animal" during hunting season brought us all elk ribs, which we cooked over the grill outside on a beautiful sunny day on the mountain. They were enormous, and some of the best ribs I've ever had. Feel free to experiment; there are no special cooking techniques required.

Chapter Four
Rib Cooking Methods

N o discussion of cooking ribs (or any type of meat for that matter) can begin without introducing you to my patented wellness guide. Actually, this time-honored method is used by chefs all over the world to test meat temperature. They'd get into a lot of trouble if they had to cut into each steak to see if it was done.

Rare

Take your index finger and press the tip of it into the web between your other index finger and thumb. See how "springy" that feels—like you can press down about three-quarters of an inch? If you push your finger into a steak and it has about the same "give," that means it's rare. Guaranteed.

Medium

Take that same tip of your index finger and poke into the little dimple under your lower lip. Kind of springy, right? A little less than a half-inch of "give." Getting that same feeling out of a steak or burger will result in a medium-rare temperature burger.

Well

Now poke yourself in the forehead. Almost no "give" to it at all. That's the feeling you're looking for when you probe (lightly) into that steak.

Obviously this is not the most scientific method available. But practice makes perfect, and soon enough you will be able to distinguish temperature almost by looking at a piece of meat on the grill. Of course, you could go the route of the meat thermometer—but that will make you look even more ridiculous than the dreaded grill knife. Practice a lot, and buy a dog if you don't already have one. That way you have a partner to eat your mistakes.

Parboiling

Ribs are oftentimes a real labor of love involving many steps, and requiring a great deal of time to prepare. You'll likely encounter recipes that call for extended periods of

marinating, and painfully slow cooking times. Taking your time slaving over the perfect rack of ribs is to be commended, but they can make ribs more of a hobby than a meal. The fact is that most of us don't have a few hours to slowly cook ribs over low heat—and fewer still have the forethought to prepare a marinade that needs to chill in the refrigerator for up to 24 hours (even before the meat is added)! That's why parboiling makes so much sense.

Parboiling is a great way to prepare your ribs for the grill while tenderizing them and infusing them with flavor at the same time. In fact, whenever you plan on quickly searing your ribs over a hot grill, I recommend parboiling them first. The "par" part is crucial; you don't actually want to fully boil your ribs. Doing so incurs the opposite of the intended effect: making your ribs tough and chewy. What you want to do is precook them slightly, let some of the excess fat boil off them, and moisten and heat them so they more readily absorb your barbecue sauce or dry rubs.

To parboil ribs (or chicken, for that matter), all you need is water, and a pot large enough to accommodate your meat. Bring the water to a steady boil, and place the meat in the pot. In the case of ribs, you can periodically skim the fat off the surface of the water. Usually no more than 10 minutes is required to completely parboil the ribs. An additional 15 minutes on the grill should get the job done. A great way to add flavor to your ribs prior to grilling is to add some seasoning to the water. I recommend adding a cup of honey, a cup of unsulphered molasses, and a cup of white wine vinegar to each gallon of water used.

After parboiling, you should let your ribs cool, and pat them dry with a towel. Then you are ready to apply your dry rub or barbecue sauce. As a general rule, I would only recommend parboiling ribs for those occasions when you simply don't have time to cook them slowly.

Grilling

As discussed earlier, grilling is probably the least preferable complete cooking method for ribs. Ribs tend to be at their best when slow-barbecued over a smoky fire for hours at a time. However, in the case of ribs that have been parboiled, grilling is necessary to sear in your sauce and seal in the flavors of a dry rub. The key to finishing off parboiled ribs is to make sure your grill surface is nice and hot, yet not allow open flames to come in contact with your meat, which will blacken the surface.

Barbecuing

The word "barbecue" is thought to be derived from the Spanish word *barbacoa*, which was, in turn, picked up from Indians. (It is unclear whether they were Native Americans or West Indians, though the *Oxford English Dictionary* traces the word's etymology back to Haiti where the practice was to slow-cook meat over hot coals.) Another etymological theory points to the French phrase *barbe a queue*, which means "whiskers to tail," and refers to the method of cooking the whole animal over a spit. Either way, to barbecue means to cook meat slowly by indirect heat. It is the preferred method of preparing ribs.

Barbecuing with a Charcoal Grill

Charcoal grills are best suited for barbecuing in the traditional sense of the word. Unlike gas grills, charcoal grills offer the added advantage of the fuel (charcoal briquettes or wood) imparting extra flavor to the meat—charcoal flavor we associate most closely with real barbecue. Any brazier-type open-flame grill can be used, but preferably one with a hood, so the smoke can stay in and the heat can be regulated.

My suggestion for any slow-cooking technique starts with the preparation of your fuel. You want to achieve a consistent ashy surface: hot even-burning coals, with a coat-

ing of white ash on top. Next, spread your coals along the outside of the grill so that the actual cooking surface you place your meat on will not be in direct contact with open flames. The key to achieving moist and tender barbecue is even, steady, indirect heat. Naturally, managing your fire becomes the greatest challenge of barbecuing.

What you are looking for is a heat, at the grilling surface, of about 225° F. Depending on the thickness of your ribs, roughly of 2 hours of indirect heat should be enough to reach an internal temperature of 170°F (the recommended minimum for pork). With a charcoal grill, the greatest challenge is to maintain a steady temperature while you are opening and closing the lid to add and move your coals/wood. This is impossible. You should expect the grill temperature to swing 50 degrees either way during the cooking process—but that's perfectly all right. You're not cooking a soufflé.

Sometimes the greatest challenge, especially on a small grill, is to keep your meat away from the flames altogether. In the case of my Weber, I like to place an old steel pan right filled to the top with water in the middle of the coal grate and organize my coals around it, leaving a fairly ample "no flame" zone in the middle of the grill. But sometimes that isn't enough to stop fat-fueled flames from coming up and searing the sides of the meat. In that case, I take heavy-duty aluminum foil and place it strategically underneath the ribs. Naturally, you will have to play around with various configurations to get your home grill to behave. Unfortunately, most "barbecues" aren't designed for the task that embodies their moniker.

Barbecuing with a Gas Grill

Even though many barbecue aficionados will rail against the gas grill, I'm here to tell you that good barbecue can be made on one. The problem most charcoal-heads out there have is the fact that gas grills take away a lot of flavor in the cooking process. What they forget to mention is the fact that, while they are slaving away adding and removing coals from their kettles, the gas grill owner is having an ice-cold Budweiser while his grill maintains a steady temperature of 225°F hour after hour.

As far as the flavor debate goes, it is clear that hardwood charcoal briquettes and natural hardwoods add a lot of flavor to the meat. However, most of the flavor comes from the fat that drips off the meat and is returned upward in the form of smoke. A good gas grill usually has lava rocks, ceramic briquettes, or (like my Weber) metal "flavor bars" that catch drippings and return ample smoke. If you really have to have that wood taste, however, you can add a tray of water-soaked wood chips underneath the grilling surface.

Smoking with a Water Smoker

Smoking is essentially barbecuing with some smoke and moisture added. Like the slow-barbecuing technique described earlier, the goal of smoking is to create a cooking environment that's about 225–250°F, and let hot, moist circulating air do the cooking, rather than the direct flame.

The process by which smoking happens is fairly simple. Regular smokers use a two-tiered pan system in which the bottom pan contains your fuel (preferably burning hardwood), with a pan of water above. The heat boils the water. The water creates a hot vapor to which the smoke naturally binds. Moist, flavored smoke circulates around your meat for several hours. The result is extremely tender and flavorful meat. Most of the commercial smokers available on the market utilize a three-tiered system of pans: the bottom pan for the fire, the middle pan for the water, and the top pan for the meat.

Covered barbecues can be turned into smokers by the simple addition of some wood chips to the fire and a pan of water above the coal surface. You can also get the effect of smoking on a regular grill by cooking your meat wrapped in a layer of heavy-duty aluminum foil with some water sprinkled inside. In the case of ribs, you can put the package of wrapped ribs inside a low-heat grill for about 1 hour, and take the foil off for another 30 minutes.

One of the great things about smoking is experimenting with different hardwoods. Most people immediately think of mesquite, but there are many wonderful hardwoods out there that add their own unique flavor. Try oak, cherry, hickory, and alder. Many of these can be found prepackaged in ready-to-use "chips" at your supermarket or specialty food store. If you can't find it in the store, you can find it in the forest.

Oven-Cooking

I spent thirty years as a city dweller so I can't ignore the fact that many of you will have to prepare your ribs in the oven. But you will be surprised at the kind of results you can get right out of your kitchen. Nothing maintains slow, steady temperature better than your oven and, with the proper technique, you can achieve near-perfect barbecued foods.

The easiest way to cook ribs in an oven is to cut a piece of heavy-duty aluminum foil that's big enough to accommodate a half rack of ribs. Cover the ribs with barbecue sauce and place in the fridge for at least 12 hours. When ready to cook, put the whole foil package in the oven and cook at 300°F for a minimum of 2 hours or until you see that the meat on the end of each rib has "shrunk back" from the bone about 1/2 inch. Remove the ribs from the foil and turn up the oven to about 400°F. Using the top rack, quickly brown the ribs on both sides for ten minutes, turning them over after about five minutes. The combination of the marinade and long cooking time should result in fairly tender ribs.

But here's another good method: First, heat your oven to about 425°F and brown your ribs for about ten minutes. The goal is to surface-cook the meat, so that the outside forms a barrier that retains moisture (the same principle as browning stew meat). Remove your browned ribs from the oven and lower the oven's temperature to 300°F. Place the ribs directly on the oven rack about 8 inches from the top of the oven. Place a pan of water below them (to catch fat drippings and prevent them from smoking you out of the kitchen). If you are using a mop, you can apply it every time the ribs appear dry. Depending on the amount and size of ribs, 2 hours of cooking should be ample, and result in very tender, meat-falling-off-the-bone ribs. Just make sure your oven doesn't get too hot.

Braising

Braising is the method by which you slow-cook ribs in a pan, simmering them in their own juices. It's very similar to making a stew, except you don't have to cut the food into even pieces, and you don't need enough liquid to cover the food.In braising, the pot is usually covered very tightly so that the meat cooks slowly in its own juices, and so that very little steam escapes. It's a technique largely favored in cooking large cuts of meat, and generally gives the meat a very tender texture, along with infusing it with lots of flavor. The leftover braising liquid is also flavorful and can be served as a sauce. Braising is also an excellent opportunity to use flavorsome but less tender cuts of meat. Try your hand at braising with the recipe Stovetop Short Ribs with Pan Sauce on page 81.

Chapter Five
Sauces, Rubs, Glazes, and Marinades

Barbecue and Grilling Sauces

Basic Barbecue Sauce

Yields approximately 3 cups

This is the all-American stuff, and can be used as a "base" for creating endless variations of sauces. I think most people will be surprised how simple and gratifying making your own barbecue sauce is, and how much fresher and better tasting it is than reaching for the bottle of Open Pit or KC Masterpiece at the supermarket.

4 tablespoons vegetable oil

1 onion, finely chopped

6 large garlic cloves, finely chopped

½ cup cider vinegar

⅓ cup Worcestershire sauce

1 ½ cups ketchup

⅓ cup brown sugar

2 teaspoons chili powder

½ teaspoon cayenne pepper

½ teaspoon cumin

Bring a medium-size saucepan to medium heat, and add the oil, letting it warm in the pan. Cook the onion and garlic slowly, browning until soft.

Meanwhile place the vinegar, Worcestershire sauce, and ketchup into a mixing bowl. Add the dry ingredients (brown sugar and spices) into the mixing bowl, stirring until blended.

Pour the mixture into the saucepan, and raise the heat until simmering. Stir often, checking for "thickness" of the sauce. The goal is to seamlessly blend the flavors together while achieving a sauce that's thick enough to stick — literally — to your ribs. For a "spicier" sauce, 1 teaspoon of Tabasco or other pepper sauce can be added.

North Carolina–Style Barbecue Sauce

Yields approximately 1 cup

Not all barbecue sauce has to be the red, tomato-based stuff most of us are familiar with. In fact, in eastern North Carolina, there is no such thing. The sauce is this spicy vinegar-based preparation, traditionally used for sliced and "pulled" pork, but equally as good for marinating ribs and as a dipping sauce.

1 cup cider vinegar

2 tablespoons salt

½ teaspoon black pepper

¼ teaspoon cayenne pepper

1 teaspoon red pepper flakes

1 tablespoon brown sugar

Mix ingredients well. Let stand. That's it! (Most folks from eastern NC recommend letting this mixture sit for as long as possible, and many keep this sauce bottled for weeks at a time, saying that it only improves the taste). A minimum of 12 hours is recommended, but you can probably get away with 3 hours.

Deep South—Mustard-based Barbecue Sauce

Yields approximately 3 cups

Just about every region of the south can claim its own type of barbecue style. This mustard-based sauce originated in the Deep South, specifically South Carolina and Georgia. It's a wonderful basting and serving sauce for any type of barbecued meat, especially sliced pork and brisket. I also like it on my ribs as a dipping sauce.

2 tablespoons unsalted (sweet) butter

1 cup yellow mustard

1/2 cup red wine vinegar

1/2 cup white wine vinegar

1/2 cup sugar

2 teaspoons salt

1 tablespoon Worcestershire sauce

1 1/2 teaspoons ground black pepper

Tabasco sauce (optional)

To prepare, heat a medium-size saucepan over medium heat, and melt the butter (to prevent other ingredients from sticking). Gradually add the rest of the ingredients into the pan, stirring until smooth. Let the mixture rise to a simmer, and lower heat. Simmer for approximately 20 minutes, and set aside to cool. This sauce can be refrigerated (if bottled or well-covered) for 2 weeks.

Traditional South American Barbecue Sauce

Yields approximately 1 1/2 cups

I know of no better barbecue sauce than South American–style. This vinegar-based, herb-infused sauce is served at most of Argentina's and Brazil's roadside *churrascaria* joints. You can use this sauce to baste meats during cooking, and serve it (at room temperature) in a bowl alongside the meal.

1 cup boiling water

8 large garlic cloves, minced finely

½ cup parsley, chopped finely

½ cup fresh oregano, chopped finely

¼ cup dried red pepper

½ cup white wine vinegar

½ cup extra virgin olive oil

1 teaspoon salt

1 teaspoon ground black pepper

This recipe is staggeringly easy to prepare. First, using a small-size pot, bring the water to a raging boil. Second, get a separate pot large enough to hold all of the ingredients. Place the garlic, parsley, oregano, and dried pepper into the pot. Pour the boiling water on top, and then add the vinegar, olive oil, salt, and pepper. Let cool for about 1 hour.

Transfer the mixture to a covered jar and store in the refrigerator for at least 24 hours to let the flavors blend. It can be stored this way for up to 14 days.

Chinese Sparerib Sauce

Yields approximately 1½ cups

There are probably about as many Asian barbecue sauce preparations as there are regional American ones. Here's the fast-and-easy way to whip up an authentic tasting Chinese–style sauce using only a modicum of effort.

1 cup ketchup

3 ½ tablespoons soy sauce

1 tablespoon liquid smoke

¾ cup brown sugar

1 tablespoon ground ginger

3 large garlic cloves, minced

Heat a medium-size pan over high heat and add all of the ingredients, stirring until well blended. Let the mixture come to a simmer and lower the heat. Stir often, until sugar is fully dissolved. The sauce is done when it becomes thick, and the sugar rises, bubbling to the surface.

Let the mixture cool. Also makes a great marinade.

Dry Rubs, Glazes, and Marinades

All-Purpose Dry Rub

Yields approximately enough for 1 rack

Almost every time I cook ribs, I season them overnight with a rub, a mixture of dry spices rubbed into the surface of the meat. "Rubbing" your ribs, and then storing them in the refrigerator overnight before cooking adds tremendous flavor, and enables you to cook the ribs for a shorter period, because you are not solely depending on the barbecue sauce to provide the flavor. Again, the varieties of rubs are as infinite as the amount of dry spices you can find in your cabinet. However, there are some basic spices that mix well, and seem to work best with ribs. Here's my favorite mixture:

1 tablespoon ground cumin

½ tablespoon chili powder

½ tablespoon kosher salt

1 teaspoon dried mustard powder

Pepper to taste (freshly ground)

Mix all ingredients together in a bowl, rub thoroughly into the meat, and refrigerate overnight in a sealed container (a plastic bag actually works best).

Want to experiment? Try adding 1 or 2 teaspoons of any of these spices to the above: cardamom, cinnamon, paprika, celery salt, onion powder, curry powder, cayenne pepper, powdered garlic, ground ginger...you get the picture. After some experimenting, you will be able to create the appropriate rub for any occasion.

All-Purpose BBQ Glaze

Yields approximately 2 cups

Glazes are thick, usually semisweet sauces that can be applied immediately before or after cooking. When you apply it after cooking, the heat of the meat serves to cook the glaze in, and gives your dish a lovely shiny, glazed appearance and a nice color. The simplest glazes can be reductions of sweet juices, such as cider. For example, boiling down a quart of apple cider until syrupy produces a wonderfully sweet apple glaze that is perfect for pork ribs or a whole roast. Here is a great all-purpose glaze for ribs or chicken dishes (I like to use alcohol in this recipe, but you can replace with water if you prefer).

1 tablespoon olive oil

3 cloves garlic, finely minced (or pressed through a garlic press)

½ cup bourbon whiskey (or dark rum if preferred)

½ cup ketchup

⅓ cup cider vinegar

1 teaspoon Worcestershire sauce

¼ cup brown sugar

¼ teaspoon dried mustard powder

½ tablespoon freshly squeezed lemon juice

Salt and pepper to taste

Place a medium-size saucepan over medium heat, and add the olive oil. Add the garlic, sauteing until slightly soft. Add the bourbon whiskey, ketchup, vinegar, and Worcestershire sauce. Blend well. Continue stirring, and add the brown sugar gradually. Add the dried mustard powder next. Continue to stir until the mixture simmers, and the brown sugar is fully dissolved. Stir in the lemon juice, add salt and pepper to taste, remove from heat, and let cool to room temperature. Store the mixture in the refrigerator until ready to use. Baste onto ribs (or chicken) before cooking, and apply a thin glaze immediately after taking off the grill. (Makes enough for two racks of baby back ribs or ten chicken pieces).

All-Purpose Rib Marinade

Yields approximately 5 cups

Cooking great ribs is like painting. It's the prep work that kills you. Once you actually get to the grill with the ribs, most of the hard work is done. One of my favorite ribs recipes requires seventy-two hours of prep time before you get to the grill, where the ribs take at least four hours to cook! That's a little hardcore for most people, but it does go a long way to illustrate just how important preparation is. One of the keys to consistently getting flavorful, tender ribs off your grill is the right marinade. This is the one I recommend.

2 12-ounce cans Budweiser (or whatever beer you're drinking)

½ cup warm water

1 cup cider vinegar

¼ cup Worcestershire sauce

¼ cup soy sauce

1 tablespoon chili powder

1 teaspoon ground cumin

1 teaspoon dried mustard powder

½ teaspoon cayenne pepper (substitute three dashes Tabasco if preferred)

1 ¾ cups brown sugar

Put a large saucepan over a high flame to preheat. While the pan is heating, combine the beer, water, vinegar, Worcestershire sauce, and soy sauce. Add to pan, and heat until boiling.

Add the dry spices and sugar, stirring to help dissolve the sugar. Once the sugar is fully dissolved, remove it from the heat (you don't want to reduce this marinade to achieve thickness–it works better thin).

Use this marinade immediately, placing ribs in a shallow roasting pan or leak-proof plastic bags. The key is to keep all of the meat in contact with the marinade, and keep air out. If you choose to use a pan, place plastic wrap or wax paper directly over the ribs. Turn them several times over a period of twelve to 24 hours.

If you are going to be the master of your own backyard barbecue domain, you have to know your sauce. Here's a prep guide for the recipes in the next chapter.

Eastern North Carolina

The sauce is vinegar-based, with spicy pepper. Usually served with sliced pork, it is especially good served with grilled ribs.

Deep South

In Georgia and South Carolina, the traditional sauce is mustard-based, rather than tomato-based. It can be thinned and used as a basting sauce and, at full strength, is a wonderful dipping sauce for ribs.

Central South (Memphis, Tennessee)

The sauce is a sweet, tangy tomato-based concoction. An important base ingredient is molasses.

Texas

The sauce is tomato-based, and spicy. Texans like lots of heat in their barbecue sauce, whether provided by chili peppers, cayenne pepper, or hot pepper sauces.

Kansas City

Thick, tangy, and sweet. You'll find lots of spices in Kansas City sauces, including cinnamon, cumin, chili powder, and garlic.

Caribbean

There are really two distinct Caribbean styles. Fruit-based sauces and glazes characterized by native heat provided by chilies make for sweet and tangy sauces. There is also the popular "jerk" style of sauce, a super hot and spicy thin sauce that employs oil, vinegar, habanero peppers, onions, and spices like cinnamon, allspice, and nutmeg.

Chapter Six
Rib Recipes

There are probably several thousand excellent rib recipes out there today, one no better than another. In fact, there are probably as many variations as there are people who make ribs. The thing to keep in mind in reading (and using) the following recipes is that they are all guidelines, and they will work best for you with experimentation. In the chapter that follows, I have attempted to put together those rib recipes that everyone should know how to prepare.

Texas-Style Baby Back Ribs

Yields 6 servings

The first, most important step in making authentic Texas-style ribs is the mop. The mop (so-called because it is usually applied with the household apparatus of the same name) is basically a marinade, basting sauce, and dipping sauce all in one. Real Texas barbecue masters are used to mopping several dozen chickens, slabs of ribs, and briskets at a time so they need an actual string mop to handle the task. You can use one of those kitchen glassware scrubbers to get the miniaturized effect.

This Texas-style mop can also be used on poultry or other meat dishes—especially brisket. I usually make lots of extra sauce when I make this recipe, and store it (refrigerated) in a clean, used mayo jar.

3 large racks, baby back ribs, excess fat trimmed and membrane removed

1 Bag medium-size mesquite chips (for outdoor grills)

Marinade and Dipping Sauce

Yields approximately 8 cups

4 tablespoons olive oil

1 cup unsalted butter

2 medium-size white onions, finely chopped

6 medium-size shallots, finely chopped

10 large cloves garlic, pressed

3 cups pureed tomatoes

12-ounce can tomato paste

12-ounce can beer

12 ounces water

6 tablespoons vinegar

4 tablespoons Worcestershire sauce

Juice of 1 lemon

6 tablespoons brown sugar

2 tablespoons chili powder

2 teaspoons dried mustard powder

2 teaspoons cumin

1 teaspoon cayenne pepper (more if desired)

Salt and pepper to taste

Heat a large sauté pan on a medium-high flame and add the olive oil. After the oil is heated sufficiently, add the butter. Sauté the onions, shallots, and garlic until transparent.

Add the rest of the liquid ingredients (pureed tomatoes,

tomato paste, beer, water, vinegar, Worcestershire sauce, and lemon juice), and heat until simmering.

Once simmering, add the dry spices, stirring in gradually. Let this mixture simmer for at least 30 minutes.

When finished (taste it—you may want to sweeten it with more sugar, or spice it up using more cayenne pepper), reserve 1 cup of the sauce for your mop, and at least 1 cup for a dipping sauce.

Place your ribs in a shallow baking pan and cover with the remainder of the mopping sauce. Try to fully submerge the ribs, and place sheets of plastic wrap or wax paper directly atop the meat, so as to eliminate air. If the ribs are not totally covered, rotate them periodically. Marinate for a minimum of 12 hours.

Mop

1 cup reserved marinade

6 ounces beer (chef's choice)

Mix the reserved marinade and beer together well, and place into a bowl.

Cook the ribs using one of the methods described in Chapter 4. I would recommend smoking these ribs with water-soaked, medium-size mesquite chips. That smoky, mesquite flavor is the signature of Texas–style barbecue.

Cantonese Pork Spareribs

Yields 4 to 6 servings

Chinese people really know how to barbecue. For me, there's nothing that gets my appetite up faster than walking down Mott Street in New York's Chinatown and seeing freshly barbecued meats hanging in the window. Passing by whole barbecued ducks, roasted pork, and gigantic racks of spareribs, it's hard to pass up the urge to go in and polish off a few dishes with an ice cold Tsing Tao.

The reason we order in—and go out for—Chinese food is because the preparation time involved in cooking it makes it inconvenient to cook at home. When it comes to spareribs, it's not uncommon for the meat to be marinated for days at a time before it is finally put on the grill.

Here is one of my favorite recipes for Chinese spareribs and, yes, it does take a bit of preparation. But once you tuck into these eminently flavorful ribs, you'll be glad you took the time to do it right.

2 good-size racks of spareribs, fat trimmed and membrane removed

Sesame seeds

Marinade

Yields about 2 cups

⅓ cup hoisin sauce

½ cup Chinese wine

4 tablespoons low-sodium soy sauce

1/3 **cup honey**

1/2 **cup minced scallion**

2 tablespoons minced fresh ginger

2 tablespoons ground bean sauce (available at Chinese grocers)

4 large cloves garlic, finely minced

1 tablespoon cider vinegar

1/2 **teaspoon curry powder**

Combine all of the ingredients in a saucepan and heat gradually over a low flame, while stirring. Do not let this come to a boil. Just heat it sufficiently to let the flavors come together. Let the mixture cool.

Put your spareribs in a shallow baking pan and cover with the marinade and refrigerate. The ribs should remain in the marinade for a minimum of 24 hours for maximum effectiveness. In fact, if you can leave them in for several days, that would be better. Remember to shift the ribs around periodically to insure all your ribs are well covered.

You can cook these ribs on the grill or oven-cook them. The grill is preferable. Remember, the endgame is to cook the ribs for at least 2 hours at a temperature of 225ºF. Also remember to reserve some of the marinade to use as a basting sauce throughout the cooking process. You should baste your ribs once every 20 minutes, or whenever they appear dry on the surface.

When your ribs are finished, you are ready to lightly brush on your glaze.

Glaze

3 tablespoons honey

2 tablespoons low-sodium soy sauce

3 teaspoons sesame seed oil

Combine the ingredients, brush on your glaze, and sprinkle sesame seeds over the top to finish it off.

Korean Short (Beef) Ribs

Yields 4 to 6 servings

Beef short ribs are generally pretty tough customers, requiring long marinating times to get them tender. I like to make them Korean–style (the traditional Korean name for them is *Bulkogi*) because there is something about the marinade that really breaks down the meat and gets them super-tender.

Another thing that's so neat about short ribs is that, because they are beef, you don't have to worry about undercooking them; they can be served rare. The other great thing about this recipe is that the only difficult part about it is having patience for the marinade—you'll need to soak them for at least 12 hours, preferably more.

6 pounds short ribs, cut into thin pieces, about 2 1/2 inches long

Marinade

Yields approximately 1½ cups

2 tablespoons toasted sesame seeds

4 large cloves fresh garlic, pressed

1 cup soy sauce

2 tablespoons sherry (or substitute sweet rice wine)

3 tablespoons sugar

2 tablespoons sesame oil

2 tablespoons water

2 teaspoons fresh ginger, finely grated

½ cup chopped green scallions (green and white portion, mixed)

Toast the sesame seeds in a regular pan, over a low flame. Remove the seeds when nicely browned, and set aside.

Combine the rest of the marinade ingredients, mixing well. Using a black pepper grinder on a fine setting, mill the toasted sesame seeds into the mix and stir in.

Add your ribs to the marinade, and let them sit in it (refrigerated) as long as you possibly can. (I like to prepare the marinade the night before, so it's ready for the next night's dinner.)

Get a hot fire on your barbecue going, and grill these ribs until they are nicely browned and crispy on the edges. Depending on the thickness of the ribs, they should take between 15–20 minutes. If you plan on cooking these in the oven, they can be roasted in a 400ºF oven for 30 minutes. Be sure to baste them often.

Kansas City–Style Dry-Rubbed Beef Ribs with KC Barbecue Dipping Sauce

Yields 4 to 6 servings

Kansas City is the crossroads of barbecue, a place where American barbecue styles melded together. The combination of transplanted Southerners and Texans, and more beef than you can shake a stick at (it is the Midwest, of course) produced a barbecue culture of its own. Both KC Masterpiece and Bull's-Eye bottled sauces came out of KC, which is testimony to its appeal.

The style of classic Kansas City sauce varies according to which part of Kansas City you're from. Generally, it is a thick, tomato-laden, tangy and sweet sauce. Pretty much like KC Masterpiece. Homemade is better, of course.

This recipe is the best of all worlds: you have a great classic dry rub and a fantastic sauce for dipping. This recipe calls for beef ribs (acknowledging Kansas City's Midwestern beef heritage—although most KC restaurants serve the traditional baby back ribs), but you can substitute whatever kind of ribs you like. I like to dry-rub my ribs first, baste some barbecue sauce on for the last 20 minutes of cooking, and use the sauce for dipping while I eat. However, feel free to thin down the (thick) sauce to use as a mop during cooking.

2 large racks of beef ribs

or 3 large racks of baby back ribs

2 large ziplocked freezer storage bags

Dry Rub

Yields about 2 cups, but good to save. It will last indefinitely

1 cup sugar

$\frac{1}{2}$ cup paprika

$\frac{1}{4}$ cup kosher salt

$\frac{1}{4}$ cup celery salt

$\frac{1}{4}$ cup garlic powder

3 tablespoons onion powder

3 tablespoons chili powder

2 tablespoons cumin

2 tablespoons ground black pepper

2 teaspoons dried mustard powder

1 teaspoon cayenne pepper

Mix ingredients together and
store in a sealed jar.

Classic Barbecue Sauce

Yields about 4 cups

1 teaspoon seasoned salt

1 teaspoon chili powder

1 teaspoon cumin

1 teaspoon mild curry powder

1 teaspoon paprika

$\frac{1}{2}$ teaspoon ground allspice

½ **teaspoon ground cinnamon**

½ **teaspoon mace**

½ **teaspoon freshly ground black pepper**

½ **teaspoon red (cayenne) pepper**

2 cups ketchup

¾ **cup dark unsulphered molasses**

½ **cup white wine vinegar**

1 teaspoon Tabasco sauce

In a large bowl, mix dry ingredients well. Add ketchup, molasses, vinegar, and Tabasco. Transfer mixture to a saucepan and heat over a medium flame until warm, stirring frequently. The idea is to make sure the dry ingredients melt into the sauce.

Buy your ribs and make your dry rub the day before you plan on cooking. To apply dry rub, sprinkle (rather than actually rub) the mixture on the meat—it should be moist enough so that the rub sticks to the surface. A light coating is sufficient, but use as much as you like, as it tends to come off during handling and cooking. Seal your ribs in plastic bags, and set in the refrigerator overnight. You can also prepare your sauce that day and set it aside.

If you are planning on barbecuing these ribs, set your temperature at roughly 250°F and cook your ribs with the lid closed. Adding some soaked mesquite or other hardwood chips is recommended, but not necessary. Cook the ribs for approximately 2 ½ to 3 hours, or until the meat has shrunk back well from the bone. About 15 minutes before the ribs are done, add a generous coating of your barbecue sauce.

Serve with the remaining sauce and ice-cold beer.

Citrus Barbecued Ribs

Yields approximately 4 to 6 servings

I think because we're so used to having ribs smothered in tomato-based sauce that we forget the simple fact that spareribs and baby backs can yield pork that is as tasty as tenderloin. Then why not serve a sauce with your ribs that's a bit more refined? In this recipe, you'll make a great citrus marinade that you can even use on chicken, and a great fruit-based glaze to finish it off.

4 pounds spareribs

Citrus Cilantro Marinade

Yields approximately 2 cups

⅓ **cup lime juice (fresh only!)**

⅓ **cup orange juice (fresh is better, but**

    Tropicana Homestyle can be substituted)

3 tablespoons fresh lemon juice

2 teaspoons grated lemon peel

2 teaspoons grated lime peel

½ **cup extra virgin olive oil**

⅔ **cup fresh cilantro, finely chopped**

4 large garlic cloves, pressed

½ **teaspoon cayenne pepper**

½ **teaspoon coarsely ground black pepper**

¼ **teaspoon kosher salt**

¼ teaspoon oregano

¼ teaspoon paprika

¼ teaspoon allspice

Tom's Red Hot (optional)

Mix all ingredients together well, and store in the refrigerator until use. I recommend marinating in this sauce for at least 4 hours, possibly more. If you like heat, you can add and subtract cayenne pepper or hot pepper sauce at will. Just add it incrementally, tasting as you go until you are satisfied with the level of heat. I happen to prefer Tom's Red Hot for this recipe, because it "adds flavor, not just heat" unlike other hot sauces, which can quickly overpower your marinade.

Orange Glaze
Yields approximately 2 cups

1 cup water

1 cup sugar

Juice of 4 large oranges

¼ cup chili sauce

2 tablespoons honey

2 tablespoons lime juice

1 teaspoon hot sauce

Combine water and sugar in the pan and simmer until reduced by half. (To insure you don't burn the sugar, heat the water first, and stir in the sugar when hot). Add the juice of the oranges, stirring it in as you go. Add the rest of the ingredients. Simmer until the mixture is about the consistency of thin maple syrup. Let it cool before you baste it on your ribs.

Cook your spareribs using one of the methods described in Chapter 4. When you remove them from the grill, brush on a light coating of the Orange Glaze, reserving some on the side to use as a dipping sauce.

Dry-Rubbed Baby Backs with Mustard Glaze

Yields approximately 4 to 6 servings

One of my favorite ways to prepare ribs is dry-rubbing, followed by the application of a tasty glaze after cooking. Allowing ribs to dry-marinate in spice adds an intense flavor to your ribs—one you can't replicate using an off-the-shelf sauce from the supermarket. This recipe will also impress your barbecue-shy friends who are used to having ribs steeped in tomato-based, Texas-type sauce. Use the following recipe as a general template for cooking any style of ribs: all you need is your favorite rub recipe, and your favorite glaze. The recipe that follows combines two of my favorite components: an extra spicy dry rub with lots of cayenne pepper for added heat and a sweet brown-sugar glaze that gives your ribs a luscious ruby-red color that reminds me of Chinese spareribs.

The preparation couldn't be simpler: rub your ribs with an ample amount of dry rub; cook over indirect heat for at least 2 hours, covered, in a 225ºF barbecue; and apply the glaze the instant the ribs come off the grill.

2 medium-sized racks ribs

Dry Rub
Yields 2 cups

1 cup brown sugar

½ cup paprika

1 tablespoon kosher salt

1 tablespoon coarsely ground black pepper

1 tablespoon powdered garlic

1 tablespoon chili powder

1 tablespoon cayenne pepper

½ tablespoon cumin

1 teaspoon white pepper

1/2 teaspoon dried mustard powder

Mix all of the ingredients well, and sprinkle liberally on ribs. Set the ribs in sealed plastic bags, and refrigerate for a minimum of 12 hours.

Glaze
Yields approximately 2 cups

2/3 cup brown sugar

½ cup red wine vinegar

½ cup honey mustard

¼ cup honey

Mix all ingredients well until sugar dissolves. Apply a thick coating on (hot) ribs immediately after removing them from the grill, so the glaze "cooks onto" the ribs.

This recipe can handle up to 6 pounds of baby backs. If you make less, store the leftover dry rub indefinitely, and the glaze for up to 2 weeks in a sealed container.

North Carolina—Style Pork Ribs

Yields approximately 4 to 6 servings

After years of eating Texas-style ribs smothered in (delicious) tomato-based barbecue sauces of every variety, I became enamored of the North Carolina-style of barbecue. This happened after a trip to Oxford, North Carolina. At the time, I was a reporter for *Tobacco International*, a pretty unglamorous tobacco industry trade journal, covering the opening of a new cigarette factory. The event was celebrated with a traditional "pig pulling," where a whole spit-roasted pig is slow-cooked to the point where the meat literally "pulls" off the carcass. It is served with a traditional vinegar-based sauce. The sauce is excellent for marinating ribs, of course, and there is a nice variation of it in which you can use, hot, to serve it.

1 rack

All-purpose Rib Marinade

Follow recipe on page 52.

Sauce

⅔ cup water

2 tablespoons sugar

1 tablespoon paprika

2 teaspoons salt

1 teaspoon black pepper

½ teaspoon dry mustard

½ **teaspoon red pepper flakes**

¼ **cup Worcestershire sauce**

⅔ **cup cider vinegar**

¾ **stick unsalted butter**

Using a small saucepan, bring the water to a boil. Add all of the dry ingredients and boil for approximately 2 minutes. Remove from the heat, and add butter, vinegar, and Worcestershire sauce. Serve warm on the side with your ribs.

Dr Pepper Ribs

Yields 4 to 6 servings

Yes, you can put just about anything into barbecue sauce, including soda pop. Sweet, syrupy yet tart cola drinks make a great base for barbecue sauces. In fact, you can look no further than the label to discover that their base ingredient is the same as many bottled sauces: corn syrup. You can substitute any type of cola in the recipe that follows, but I happen to like Dr Pepper. I can't think of any more all-American recipe, or one that achieves the delicate balance between spicy and sweet in a more unique way. Plus, it's unbelievably simple to prepare.

2 racks ribs: baby or spareribs

Sauce

Yields approximately 3 ½ cups

1 tablespoon butter

1 cup finely chopped onion

1 12-ounce can Dr Pepper

1 ½ cups ketchup

¼ cup cider vinegar

¼ cup Worcestershire sauce

1 teaspoon chili powder

1 teaspoon cumin

½ teaspoon salt

½ teaspoon black pepper

½ teaspoon cayenne pepper

2 dashes Tabasco sauce

In a medium saucepan, melt the butter and sauté the onions until translucent, about 5 minutes. Add the remaining ingredients and bring to a boil. Reduce heat until mixture is simmering, and cook covered for 25 to 35 minutes until the sauce reaches a nice, thick consistency.

Apply to ribs during the last half hour of cooking, and use remainder for a dipping sauce.

Jerk-Rubbed Island–Style Baby Backs with Mango Glaze

Yields approximately 2 to 4 servings

This recipe combines two of my favorite dishes into one: hot Jamaican–style jerk ribs and sweet Caribbean–style ribs. The result is the wonderful combination of spicy and sweet with a tang reminiscent of the islands.

2 whole racks babybacks, fat trimmed and membrane removed

Jerk Rub
Yields approximately 1 cup

2 dried habanero chilies, ground

¼ cup onion powder

1 teaspoon cinnamon powder

1 teaspoon nutmeg

½ teaspoon paprika

½ teaspoon salt

½ teaspoon black pepper

½ teaspoon allspice

Glaze
Yields approximately ½ cup

3 tablespoons mango chutney

2 tablespoons mustard

2 tablespoons apricot marmalade

Mix dry rub ingredients together well and apply to ribs. Cover in plastic bags and set in refrigerator for 1 hour. Mix glaze ingredients and set aside in small bowl.

Place ribs in preheated 225ºF oven for 1 ½ to 2 hours. Before removing, set oven on broil. Apply glaze and broil ribs for 5 minutes, meat side up — or until glaze has darkened substantially.

Stove Top Short Ribs with Pan Sauce

Yields approximately 2 to 4 servings

The great thing about short ribs is that, because they are beef, they can be prepared any endless number of ways. On the rare occasion that I don't feel like firing up the barbeque (ice storms, hurricanes) and I'm making ribs, I'll braise them on the stovetop. Braising short ribs is just like making a beef stew, and infinltely easier.

Flour

2–3 pounds short ribs, cut into small pieces (3 inches each)

4 tablespoons olive oil

2 tablespoons butter

1 large onion, chopped

3 large cloves garlic, minced finely

2 teaspoons Herbes de Provence

¾ cup beef stock

Salt and pepper to taste

Get a dinner plate and pour some flour on it. Take the ribs and coat each piece lightly in the flour.

While you are doing this, be sure to get a large skillet nice and hot. Add 2 tablespoons of the olive oil to the skillet and brown your ribs on all sides, searing the flour onto the beef—this forms a protective layer around the meat that allows it to tenderize in the pan. Remove ribs, and set aside. Scrape the pan, and reserve 2 tablespoons in a small dish to use for pan sauce later.

Clean your skillet out, and put it over a medium-high flame. Add the rest of the olive oil (another 2 tablespoons), and the butter. Sauté the onions and garlic in the pan until the onions are translucent and the garlic is soft. Spread the onions in a layer throughout the pan, and place the ribs on top. Add the herbes de provence (substitute any herbs you prefer), and pour in the beef stock. Simmer over medium heat for approximately 1 hour, or until the ribs are fork-tender.

Pan Sauce
Yields approximately 2 cups

1 tablespoon olive oil

4 tablespoons unsalted butter

Beef drippings (reserved from browning the short ribs)

1 cup red wine

½ cup beef broth

½ teaspoon flour

Heat a small saucepan over a medium flame and add olive oil and butter. Next, add the pan scrapings you reserved from braising the ribs. Stirring well, add the red wine and beef broth. Thicken by whisking in flour. Serve warm with ribs.

Drunken Chicken

Yields approximately 2 to 4 servings

Okay, so these aren't exactly ribs, but I'm including this recipe because you need something to cook on that off night when you're not tending to your backyard pit. I learned this recipe from an Alabama man who I met hunting in New Mexico. There's nothing to it, and it will shock and amaze your friends who are unfamiliar with it.

1 whole chicken (fresh from the butcher if possible)

1 plastic bag big enough to hold the chicken

1 12-ounce can of light beer

Marinade/Mop

Yields approximately 2 cups

⅓ cup lemon juice (fresh only!)

⅓ cup orange juice

3 tablespoons fresh lime juice

½ cup extra virgin olive oil

1 teaspoon garlic powder

½ teaspoon cayenne pepper

½ teaspoon coarsely ground black pepper

¼ teaspoon kosher salt

¼ teaspoon oregano

¼ teaspoon paprika

Mix all of the marinade ingredients together.

Remove the gizzards from the chicken, and place the entire chicken in a plastic bag. Pour in the marinade, reserving plenty for mopping.

Squeeze all the extra air out of the bag, seal tightly, and place in the fridge overnight.

When ready to cook, preheat your grill to 350°F. Open a can of beer and place it in the middle of a roasting pan. Open the chicken's rump enough to accommodate the beer can, and gently (or not so gently, to be honest) place the can into the chicken's cavity. The idea is to have the chicken stand up on the can. Transfer the carefully balanced bird to the grill in the pan, and place the bottom of the can (holding the chicken) directly on the grill. Why? The beer will boil inside the can throughout the cooking process (light beer seems to work best, as it's more bubbly) and automatically marinate the chicken from the inside! Be sure to also apply the marinade-mop diligently (about every 15 minutes). I guarantee this will be the most moist and flavorful chicken you'll ever eat! Feel free to substitute any marinade, or use a store-bought one.

Chapter Seven
Prepared Sauces

et's face it. Unless you're a real barbecue nut, most of the time you're going to use a bottled sauce on your ribs. There's absolutely nothing wrong with that. In fact, it always surprises me that more cookbooks don't just acknowledge the fact that most of us don't have the time to "reserve sauce and chill for at least 48 hours." Most of us don't know what we're going to be doing in two hours, much less what's going to be for dinner in two *days*! We all take shortcuts when we cook, and when it comes to barbecue sauces, there are plenty of folks out there whose very job is to wait a few days—or weeks—for a barbecue sauce to blend.

Right now, there are literally hundreds of different barbecue sauces on the market. What follows are ten different ones that are readily available and represent a nice cross section of what's out there to choose from. Some you know, and can easily be found at your local supermarket. Others may require a trip to your local gourmet shop. Still others are harder to find; these are local products that can be acquired by mail or over the Internet. Some day, some real barbecue nut will rate them all like wine. Until then, I hope you enjoy this snapshot of prepared sauces, and have fun finding new ones on your journeys.

Kraft Original Barbecue Sauce

Factors: "slow simmered" and "America's favorite brand!"
Ingredients of note: Red 40

Kraft may well be "America's favorite brand," so I'm not sure if the slogan on the bottle's neck specifically refers to the company, or the barbecue sauce. However, it can't be far from the truth; this stuff sells by the gallon, and there are few of us who haven't had a piece of chicken that wasn't smothered in the stuff. I think this brand does more to anger the true Southern barbecue man than any other because of the instructions on the back of the bottle: "Pour on meat during last 15 minutes of barbecuing!" It kind of bumps up against the whole romantic notion of mopping on carefully crafted homemade sauce for hours at a time.

The dirty little secret, however, is that the stuff tastes pretty decent! Maybe it's the over-ambitious rendering of the slow-simmering pot on the label, but the miracles of food engineering make Kraft not a bad choice for those times you have to slap a coating of sauce on at the last minute. Because it's fairly inexpensive I like to use it as a base for making a quick and dirty mopping sauce for chicken—just add some beer and your favorite spices.

Where: Your local supermarket

Open Pit Original Barbecue Sauce

Factors: "authentic taste for 40 Years"
Ingredients of note: "Artificial Tomato Flavor"

Unlike the Kraft offering that doesn't try to hide its mass-market pedigree, Open Pit takes a stab at embracing the "specialty foods" side of the supermarket aisle with its distinctive packaging and inviting, rich-looking sauce. You can detect the presence of spices in the sauce, although the label merely indicates the addition of "spice." But that's okay, because I happen to like Open Pit a lot.

It really is a great all-around sauce—the label invites you to "pour," "dip," and "brush" this sauce on everything but the family pet. And why not? The stuff is tasty, especially as a substitute for ketchup on a freshly grilled hamburger. What I like about Open Pit the best is that the company actually invites us to "add onion, pepper, honey, brown sugar, or garlic to make your own special sauce." Now that's pretty cool.

Where: Your local supermarket

Bull's-Eye Original BBQ Sauce

Factors: "Straight shootin' no nonsense barbecue sauce"

Ingredients of note: "natural hickory smoke flavor"

Like its supermarket brethren, Bull's-Eye depends on lots of high fructose corn syrup, vinegar, and tomato puree as its base ingredients. In other words, it has that typical "supermarket sauce" taste; you pretty much know what to expect when you buy it. However, Bull's-Eye's bottle neck boasts a "big bold taste!" and it delivers on its promise with well-integrated flavors of hickory, onion, garlic, and a hint of mustard.

I like to have some Bull's-Eye around for dipping chicken into, and as a substitute for ketchup on hamburgers. The price makes it the perfect sauce for that Saturday barbecue when you have to grill multiple racks of ribs for a picnic and don't have the time to "whip up" a few gallons of gourmet mopping sauce. The Texas-based company makes a very flavorful Spicy Honey and Mesquite edition as well.

Where: Your local supermarket

Lea & Perrins Original BBQ Barbecue Sauce

Factors: "Extra rich, stays on thick"
Ingredients of note: Lea & Perrins Worcestershire Sauce

I love Lea & Perrins. Without them, nobody in America would be able to pronounce the word "worcestershire," much less spell it. For the last several years the company has been finding ways to market the pedigreed sauce, putting it into a proprietary steak sauce, and other company's products—including bloody mary mixes. However, if there's a natural use for this stuff, it's in a barbecue sauce, and there it stands out as one of the best mass-market blends.

It's not really a far cry from the other bottles on the supermarket shelf in terms of ingredients and general composition. However, it's quite a bit thicker and makes no bones about utilizing plenty of its parent product to create its flavor. Basically, if you like their worcestershire sauce, you'll like the BBQ sauce. To be honest with you, I like this better than their steak sauce for steaks and burgers. It is really thick, so if you're using it on chicken or ribs, I would recommend applying it for the last 15 minutes of cooking rather than using it as a mopping sauce. If you want to use it as a base for your mopping sauce, just thin it with beer, vinegar, and water so you can apply it throughout the cooking process.

Where: Your local supermarket

Honeycup Uniquely Sharp BBQ Sauce

Factors: "Product of Canada"
Ingredients of note: brown sugar

Here's another barbecue sauce that's a spin-off of a popular parent product: Honeycup's outstanding Honey Mustard Sauce. I fell in love with Honeycup Honey Mustard a long time ago, and have been smearing the stuff on ham sandwiches ever since. I never thought to add it to one of my barbecue sauce recipes, though.

Despite the company's popularity, the Honeycup barbecue sauce manages to maintain its gourmet, small-batch quality. The principle ingredient of this sauce is brown sugar, which is an excellent sign. It also uses real tomato paste, rather than the tomato purees (paste with water added) that most of the supermarket brands use. Subtle flavors of hickory, garlic, and paprika manage to blend with the principle flavor: that of the honey mustard itself. This sauce somehow manages to capture the tangy sweetness of a Deep South mustard-based sauce with the traditional Texas–style sauce in a wonderful way. Pretty incredible, considering it's made in Canada, a country not known for its barbecue.

Where: Your local gourmet store
   Or write to:
   Stone County, Inc.
   1933 Leslie Street
   Don Mills, Ontario
   CANADA M3B 2M3

Aunt Jenny's Kick'n Butt Barbecue Sauce

Factors: "Aunt Jenny" depicted on label sporting unusual haircut

Ingredients of note: coriander, cayenne pepper

I found this sauce in my local Waldbaums, but it might as well be sold in a high-priced gourmet-food store, such is the attention to detail that Aunt Jenny brings to her sauce. The clear bottle reveals a myriad of rich spices, including minced onion, parsley, and red pepper. Unseen, but evident in tasting, are: coriander, cayenne pepper, lemon peel, and garlic. A nice dose of hot sauce and mesquite liquid smoke add heat and ample flavor to round off the mix.

What I like best about this sauce is that it's thin, so you can marinate in it and apply it as a mop to ribs, chicken, or even strip steaks. Aunt Jenny doesn't mind telling you that she uses ketchup, Dijon mustard, and worcestershire sauce in her recipe. In fact, you could probably whip up something similar just by going down the list of ingredients on the label. And that's a good sign. You can't do that with a lot of mass-produced sauces: where are you going to find blue #1 and sodium benzoate? But you want to be careful about stealing Aunt Jenny's secret recipe. If she looks anything like she does on the label in real life, she could probably kick your butt.

Where: Your local supermarket

Hoboken Eddie's Specialties Homemade BBQ

Factors: " Chef like nobody's business."
Ingredients of note: "cajun spice"

Willie (the man responsible for these gorgeous photos you're flipping through) bought this stuff at a gourmet shop in New York City one day, probably because the pint-bottle packaging reminded him of a bottle of bourbon, and his subconscious mind took over. I was pretty skeptical at first, noting the trendy, retro, minimalist packaging and $7.00 price tag. Who the hell is this "Hoboken Eddie," anyway? I guess you have to be from New Jersey to know.

My skepticism ended after I tasted a fingerfull of the stuff. It is as good an example of tomato-based barbecue sauce as I've had, without resorting to using every ingredient under the sun. It has seven ingredients, each of which compliment each other perfectly: tomato puree, worcestershire and soy sauces, vinegar, brown sugar, cajun spice, and hickory smoke. That's it. No xanthan gum here. The label says that it's "brewed to a bubbling crude," and it definitely is. The only way you get seven ingredients to come together so well is slow-cooking. You can easily make this sauce yourself, but where are you going to find a spare 5 or 6 hours? Spend the $7.00 and be happy. This is a great sauce.

Where: Your gourmet-food store
  Or call:
  Hoboken Eddie's Products
  (201) 653-8080

Mad Dog Original BBQ Sauce

Factors: "nearly addictive"
Ingredients of note: tamari, unsulphered molasses

Since my "real" job involves marketing, I'm usually not one to fall prey to a gimmicky label and slick ad copy—especially when it comes to food products. That's why I was so pleasantly surprised when my old friend and barbecue master, Tim Coleman, brought this sauce to my attention. I was skeptical when I read the label's claim that the sauce "jazzes up any meal—from chicken to tofu!" (Hell, anything would "jazz up" tofu.) But, the guys who make this sauce are from a suburb of Boston, so I guess you have to expect that kind of thing.

The label also claims the stuff is "nearly addictive" and, after working my way through half a rack of grilled short ribs using Mad Dog as a dipping sauce, I'm inclined to agree. It's an all-natural sauce, made from a minimum amount of quality ingredients like real molasses, garlic, and mysterious "herbs and spices." It's also very thick and chunky, leaving a very pleasant, tangy aftertaste of tamari and heat. What I like best about it is that it is one of the few sauces that's thick, but can be used as a mop without producing a gooey, gluey mess of your ribs.

Write:

Mad Dog
Box 306
1085 Commonwealth Ave.
Dedham, MA 02215

Chubby's Grillmaster Gourmet (Medium) Barbeque Sauce

I bought this stuff after seeing it on the Internet for two reasons. First, it is the only sauce I've ever seen which spells "barbeque" with a "q" instead of a "c." (Okay, so it's a quirk, but I'm entitled). Second, the label has an awesome picture of a bib-wearing pig licking his chops on the label. Call me simple, but something about the irony of seeing a pig (who is cooked already, and about to be smoth-ered in sauce) getting ready to chow down makes me hysterical.

But what about the sauce itself? First, old Chubby doesn't pretend to be a gourmet sauce; it has very simple ingredients (corn syrup, sugar, tomato paste, soy sauce, vinegar, molasses, and spices), and it's available in a half-gallon jug. It's not a good dipping sauce either, because it's too thin. But that's what makes it great! The sauce has just the right "oomph" and consistency for mari-nating ribs (or chicken, for that matter) and using as a baste during the cooking process. It has a per-fect balance between sweet and spicy, and— incredibly—does indeed "make a great addition to your favorite meatloaf recipe" as the label claims. (I tried it.)

But who's kidding who? You're going to buy it because of the cool-looking pig on the label.

Where:

**Chubby's Sauces
Greenfield, MA 01301
www.chubbysauce.com
chubbys@shaysnet.com**

Stubb's Spicy Bar-B-Q Sauce

Factors: "Ladies and gentlemen, I'm a cook"
Ingredients of Note: anchovies, mustard flour

I found this sauce at my local supermarket, and for a very reasonable price (around $3.00 for an 18-ounce bottle). Its proprietor, C. B. Stubblefield (or "Stubby") is just about the personification of barbecue, a gregarious, yet serious-looking black Texan sporting a cowboy hat. After years of running restaurants in and around Austin, Texas, Stubbs has bottled his locally famous sauce for the masses to enjoy. He likes to say, "my life is in these bottles," and his contention is backed up by what amounts to being a classic example of Texas-style sauce with a little of his own personality thrown into the mix.

The moderately thick sauce is spicy, but not overly so, and key flavors of anchovy and tamarind announce themselves subtly without dominating what is really an excellent textbook Texas-style sauce. Stubbs recommends a three-step approach to using his products: rubbing the meat generously with his (excellent) Bar-B-Q Rub before cooking; basting with his (very good) Stubb's Moppin' Sauce while cooking; and pouring on plenty of Stubb's Bar-B-Q Sauce before serving.

Where:

Stubb's Legendary Kitchen, Inc.
PO Box 4941
Austin, TX 78765
(512) 480-0203
www.stubbsbbq.com

Other Great Sauces

Lize Jamaican Style Barbecue Sauce

The creation of Sylvia Elizabeth F "while working for a wealthy family in Long Island, N.Y.," this Jamaican rendition of traditional barbecue sauce uses honey, orange juice, and hot peppers to add a spicy tang to meats and chicken.

PO Box 128291
St. Alban, NY 11412

Oak Hill Farms Vidalia Onion Barbecue Sauce

Sweet Georgia Vidalia onions and hickory flavoring give this Atlanta-based sauce a sweet and tangy kick. This sauce is surprisingly short in calories (only 20 in 2 teaspoons, compared to up to 80 in other sauces), but long on taste. Definitely an onion lover's sauce.

Oak Hill Farms
3264 McCall Drive
Atlanta, GA 30340

Vine Star Cabernet Grilling Sauce

Cabernet wine and balsamic vinegar provide the punch that makes Vine Star stand up to rich meats like game, but subtle enough to be used as a glaze on beef. Keep the nice mason jar to store your own homemade sauces after you're done with it.

Vine Star Products
Buellton CA 93427
(877) 477-8500

Richard's Vermont–Made Mild Barbecue Sauce

Ben and Jerry's meets barbecue. One of the better mild sauces on the market, because this one actually has some flavor to it. Richard says you can "refrigerate up to one year after opening," but it will be gone before then, trust me.

Richard's Sauces
St. Albans, VT 05478

Index